LESBIAN ETIQUETTE

LESBIAN ETIQUETTE

humorous essays
by
GAIL SAUSSER

cartoons
by ALICE MUHLBACK

The Crossing Press/Trumansburg, New York 14886
The Crossing Press Feminist Series

Copyright © 1986 by Gail Sausser
Cartoons © 1986 by Alice Muhlback
Cover and book design by Martha J. Waters
Typesetting by Martha J. Waters

Printed in the U.S.A.

Library of Congress Cataloging-in-Publication Data

Sausser, Gail.
    Lesbian etiquette.

(The Crossing Press feminist series)
    1. Lesbians--United States--Anecdotes, Facetiae,
satire. I. Title. II. Series.
HQ75.6.U5S38 1986   306.7'663'0207   86-4180
ISBN 0-89594-197-X
ISBN 0-89594-196-1 (pbk.)

Thank you to my wife for love and support.
Thank you Danette Leonhardi for being my best friend.
Thank you to my old housemates for giving me Felix.
This book is for you.

Contents

Lesbian Etiquette

WE HAVE OUR own standard of etiquette within lesbian culture. It is not a formal code that says, "The Butch sleeps on the right," but a standard of norms we have developed to deal with our own particular social tensions. To paraphrase Miss Manners, "Manners are the social grease that keep us from killing one another."

We do have issues to be tense about—coming out to our parents, keeping our jobs, not getting evicted from our homes, to name a few. And if Swartz is right about lesbians having less sex than either straights or gay men, that accounts for even more tension. (But I think she interviewed the wrong lesbians. I have one friend who could have singlehandedly tipped the scales.)

The strictest code we live by is not to expose anyone else's sexual identity to the straight world. We often know one another by nicknames or only first names and people are vague about where they work. A friend once quipped that intimacy in the lesbian community meant knowing people "on a last name basis."

Lesbians are known for their rules about the proper use of language. A friend winced when she was told that since she calls herself a gay woman, not a lesbian, she is not "woman loving." Three of her lovers begged to differ. We can call ourselves dykes, but no one else

The strictest code we live by is not to expose anyone else's sexual identity to the straight world.

can and, nowadays, butch and femme refer to someone's mood or wearing apparel.

One of my friends sleeps with her best friend's ex on alternate weekends as a secondary lover, unless it's the softball season. This relationship shows how hard it is to define lesbian relationships to others. Our relationships don't fall into handy categories and that can cause us to suffer a certain confusion. I have squirmed through many a night wondering if I was on a date or if we had just gone out as friends, and wasn't willing to ask. My confusion extends to couples: are they monogamous? Are they just fighting or are they broken apart? I can't tell and sometimes neither can they.

In the absence of standard punctilio we have created the idea of primary and secondary relationships (although I'm not certain if a third becomes a second secondary, tertiary, or simply et. al.). We have coined the term "serial monogamy." And I believe that lesbians, in search of new definitions have been more willing to try experiments in relating. One woman I knew had a missionary's zeal for the cause of sleeping equally with all her "sisters." She has moved to another state now. I was merely a stopping point on a greater mission.

There are zillions of subdivisions among us from the various forms of Lesbians Against Everything to the informal sisterhood of lesbian bellydancers. Of course, we don't all think alike and have the same politics. Hoping for this is, at best, a denial of reality. But the largest gap seems to be based less on politics or ideas than on style of dress. There are those who wear the standard identifiable lesbian clothes: jeans, flannel and an assortment of sports gear as if they were prepared at any moment to scale a mountain, and there are those who wear blazers, make-up, and dresses and often do not wish to be identifiable. The "professionals" are portrayed as stuck-up, materialistic, clique-ridden, and generally Republican. The sports types are portrayed as hostile, Socialist, and menial in their occupations. Actually, having been in both camps, I am hard put to take these distinctions seriously. They are simply visual stereotypes.

Remember Lily Tomlin's famous joke that: "In the 1950s no one was gay, only shy?" The lesbian professional organization I belong to recently found, in a survey of their members, that most of them had a hard time meeting others or feeling like they fit in. It's an old story to lesbians in general. How do we cope with a hostile world, from which many of us keep very deep secrets about ourselves, and still remain capable of open arms and sharing with women we just met?

To overcome this, another woman and I decided to start a cult of friendliness. We, The Terminally Friendly, decided we would take action against The Shy who are prone to take on rejection in any form. We promised that at every lesbian function we would leap from table to table, grins wide, pumping hands and invading little coveys of fascinating, but as yet unknown, women. It's much harder than I had anticipated. Not because people are cold; just the opposite, it's because I'm shy. But I have kept a promise I made to myself to meet at least one person or couple I don't know at each function. If you wish to join The Terminally Friendly, you need only do the same.

By the way, to clear up one final note on lesbian etiquette. The butch doesn't always sleep on the right—she sleeps anywhere she damn well pleases.

The Crush

I HAD JUST met her. My palms sweated, my heart audibly pounded. Every time she came near me I giggled, stammered and apologized for myself. In an effort to regain control I tried to find faults in her. It was too late: she had none.

On our second date I found out that she was an avid mountain climber. I began to read books on climbing and suggested that we scale Mount Rainier. It was after we had dated a month and I was standing in a sporting goods store examining ice picks, that I remembered something critical—I'm afraid of heights. Ever since early childhood I've been phobic in high places, but here I was, considering dangling my body thousands of feet in the air with nothing but a rope and this ice pick. No way!

It was on that day the crush broke. She no longer seemed infallible. I began criticizing her in my mind. A week later I couldn't understand what I ever saw in her and swore I'd never have another crush again.

The perfect relationship and a soul mate found across a crowded room are the delusional qualities of a condition I get as regularly as others suffer the common cold: the crush. I get crushes more often in the spring when my hormones are raging, which leads me to believe I may someday grow out of making a fool of myself.

The Crush

However, since it seems to hit even my postmenopausal friends, I'm not so sure.

People seem to enter into love by two major methods. I call them "Kaboom" and "Friendship." There are subtle variations of each, such as "Delayed Kaboom" in which you can't stand the person the first time or two you meet them, then "Kaboom!"

"Kaboom" is the crush—the glazed-over dream of sugary sweetness that makes our friends gag as we tell them for the twentieth time about our person. "And then she looked deep into my eyes and touched my hand. What do you think it means?"

When a friend of yours is in this condition, the only safe thing to do is say, "Yes, I'm sure so and so is wild about you." Even if you're wrong and it blows up in your friend's face, she'll think you were just led astray like she was. Under no circumstances say: "Aren't you over-reacting? Maybe she just wants to be friends." Such an affront to someone's dreams is rarely forgiven, especially if you are right.

"Kaboom" either grows into friendship or disillusion but more often the latter, because of the random way in which it attacks.

"Friendship" is a more dignified way of forming a relationship. Such relationships are less stormy and, unless you like life in a soap opera, more enduring. Friendships happen without a seizure of blind passion. They are built on mutual knowledge and a shared basis of wants and needs. You begin to notice what nice eyes the person has, how sunshine glows in her hair, and how nice it is to be together. You realize you have a lot in common or that your interests complement one another's. Often, friendships survive, even when sex doesn't.

A few years ago I stabilized a ladder at midnight while a friend of mine, dressed in pink tights and a cape and holding a rose between her teeth, climbed on to a fire escape. She climbed to the third story window of a woman she had a crush on, tapped on the glass, and presented the rose. It was Valentine's Day. It didn't work out, but they are still friends.

We seem to be unusually embarrassed by crushes. In a brief survey I've just completed, few women would admit whom they had a crush on, but only one claimed she didn't get them. (She lied; I know better.) As long as they are unrequited and unknown, crushes can go on for years (they never get tested in reality that way). Many of us live in dread of our person finding out. In my case, my behavior always makes it obvious. (I don't like unrequited things.)

Signs of a crush: prolonged eye contact without hearing a word the person is saying, flying to New York to have lunch with them, sending cards and flowers, changing your plans so you "accidentally" run into them, hot flashes, stammering, clumsiness, inability to speak, and, in severe cases, swooning. There's more: obsessive thoughts, naming your cat after them, keeping their notes to you enshrined, and general paralysis, to name only a few.

Whether you call yourself swept away, caught up, obsessed, in love, in lust, glazed over, attracted to, got the hots for, starry eyed, wound up, in heat, wild about, crazy over, moon swept, dying for, pixilated, or "sugar cravin'" as Aunt Pansy used to say, chances are, you have your share of crushes. At worst they are embarrassing and at best they make you feel vulnerable and romantic.

I'd like someone to come to my window some Valentine's Day—my address is available.

8

The Dating Game

I GREW UP in a small town. I was a passive resister to boy's advances. They never interested me much beyond being a measure of status: every girl needed a Surrealistic Pillow album, white go-go boots and a boyfriend. Yet, one did not speak to boys first, call them, pick them up or pay their way. One waited to be noticed, sometimes a long time. I waited and ended up with good old Alfred, a French kisser who made saliva run down my neck.

Recently, in a rap group, we were discussing our past relationships and I found that, in overwhelming numbers, we were the seduced, not the seducers, even with other women. If so few of us initiate, how do we ever manage to get into relationships? I have made, I admit, a few bold attempts at assertiveness, but they didn't work well for me. And those lovers who did come on to me had to beat through a barrier of "Who me? Really?" Men, I assume, are out to get me. Women, I assume, are friends unless proven otherwise. It's my training.

Most of my relationships have grown tentatively out of friendships. I wait until we nearly fall all over each other panting before I say, "Uh . . . I'm attracted to you." Sometimes I never sense the right approach and that's how I've ended up with some of the deepest, most frustratingly celibate friendships of my life.

Some things . . . were never meant to be.

More than once I've waited until I was too desperate before making a move and then I've chosen lonely, alienating places like bars to meet women. Women sense the grip of neediness and resist it with fear. (It seems true that once you can live without a relationship, you are ready for one.)

An old flame told me the secret to seducing women is to show attention, compliment them, make them interested in you . . . but say no. It disarms them and captures their fantasies. Since she was able to seduce the entire cheerleading squad of her high school, I thought the method was worth a try.

I just happened to be living with an ex-cheerleader. She was straight, but experimental enough to be curious. I did say no to her continuously, and day by day it did seem to inspire her to great affection, even racy notes and persistent pleas. On the night she climbed into my bed with me and, overwhelmed, I finally said yes, she decided it was too soon. My advisor says I should have let her safely stay the initiator. I told my advisor that obviously some things were never meant to be.

I envy persistence and the ability to withstand rejection, both excellent qualities in the dating game. I have built up my courage over long hours and finally dialed the number for a date, only to be told she is busy. The agony of calling her a second and third time grows exponentially. And even when she does agree to go out with me the doubts still remain; is she only being polite?

I must have missed some of the mysterious and hidden clues of the dating game along the way. One woman I went out with wouldn't get out of the car for several minutes when I pulled up in front of her apartment building. All she would do was sit there silently. How was I to read that? Was I supposed to kiss her? Ask her out again? Ask her if the door was stuck? Since I hardly knew her, I couldn't guess what she wanted . . . and I was too nervous to know what I wanted.

Although I envy assertiveness, I don't have the indiscriminate sexual desire some others seem to. In fact, when I first came out, I was in the awkward position of knowing I was gay, but not seeing any women I was particularly attracted to. A photo of Rita Mae Brown gave me hope. I decided that somewhere out there, there was a funny, smart, beautiful lesbian capable of loving me.

It took me a while to realize that women don't run away when I tell them that they are beautiful or when I tell them that I care about them. I also enjoy it when women are attracted to me . . . as long as they aren't breathing down my neck. Dating is not as deadly serious now as it was when I first came out. Occasionally, I can even laugh at my awkwardness. And when you are both making up the rules as you go along, a sense of humor is a survival quality.

Classified Ads Can Lead
To The Real Thing

WHEN I FIRST placed an ad in a gay paper to meet other women with whom I shared the same activities I received a letter from a straight man, a letter from a drug dealing alcoholic, a letter from a retired prostitute turned kept woman, and a note from a former city council member (including press clippings) who wanted to lick my feet. Now, I ask you, where else could I have met such a diversity of people? This experience taught me the ground rules of placing an ad: never give them your address, meet in a public place during the day, and don't assume anything anyone is telling you is the truth.

There is no getting away from the fact that meeting someone from an ad is the blindest of blind dates. And there is no getting around the fact that the purpose of an ad for most people is to find a relationship—soon. The tension is nerve wracking.

First you select a sane sounding letter, then make a phone call to agree on a meeting place. (Trust me, a voice is not a good indication of character or appearance.) You describe one another so recognition is possible. I usually begin by saying, "I have curly brown hair with wisps of gold in it, deep blue eyes; I'll be wearing a tight blue cashmere sweater and a skirt slit up the side. I'll be reading *Cosmo* in the bar." (This eliminates the hard line political types.) They, of course, describe

There is no getting away from the fact that meeting someone from an ad is the blindest of blind dates.

themselves in an equally lavish way; then we both discover the truth.

At your first meeting it's wise to avoid the topic of how insanely jealous and violent your ex-lover still is, or how deeply depressed and lonely you are, or how you always carry a gun. All of these topics are a definite turn off. Only persist in religious or political topics if the person you have met is a believer too. Do not offer personality tests or ask them to join the Hunger Project. These are only suggestions.

Some say my first ad was too optimistic, but it helped me formulate what I was looking for. It read: "Wanted: beautiful, brilliant, sensuous woman in her thirties, independently wealthy and mature, who owns a business with a trainee position for me doing artistic work in a public position with low stress, high pay and immediate advancement; a woman who owns a white Mercedes sports car which she wants to give away, and who will alternately lavish me with money, love, sex and attention and leave me fully independent the rest of the time."

When I didn't get any answers I learned to write my ads more realistically and I met some people who eventually became my good friends, notably the kept woman and the straight man. I can write to the kept woman only on a certain day of the week so that she can be sure to intercept my letters while her lover is at work. She has been a stimulating pen pal. And, honestly, the straight man only wrote to me because we share the same artistic passions. Although I was warned that I would be raped, used, insulted, and an armed guard of separatists was offered, I trusted my instincts and found him to be a (perhaps rare) nice guy.

I encourage the writing of ads. Not only have I met

interesting people, but there is the ego gratification to be had when you open up your mailbox and find lots of letters from people who want to meet you. I spread them all out on the floor and walk around deciding whom to call and picturing romantic scenarios with beautiful women. I use my book of handwriting analysis. Bold sexy loops and perfumed letters get an immediate response. Small, light, squarish handwriting obviously means someone too uptight for me. The computer printout with my name typed in—a definite no. The made up wimmin's name Sponge Mossyrock is also a no. Here's an intriguing one from Rita Mae Brown, she says she's a writer too . . . hmm. Oops . . . my fantasies are getting out of hand. . . .

Ways To Dump Your Lover

I DIDN'T COME into the relationship with "reasonable expectations." I came in on a cloud of romanticism, two weeks after a break-up. I don't know why I expected the end to be rational. (She said I was unlike all the others, the love of her life; only one month after we met, and I *believed* her.)

There was evidence for some months that the end was in sight. I could feel her mind drifting. In the middle of a kiss, she'd suddenly ask, "Did the mail come?" About this time she began to be very busy at all hours. Instead of saying it was over, she began using euphemisms like, "I'm confused"; "I need space"; "Let's give it time"; and "Whatever happens, you'll be special."

These words sent me right into the compromise stage (sometimes known as the "I'll do anything" stage). If she hated my friends, I'd get rid of them; yes, all right, she could have other lovers; if necessary, I *could* get by seeing her less often.

The compromise stage is bad but, beyond doubt, the stage before I really decide it's over is the truly painful one. Tired of diving in and out of rejection, I have been known to scream, "I don't care if you want to be with me or not, just decide!" Of course, I was giving her all the power. I should have come to my own conclusion, but I just couldn't force myself to get rid of this beauti-

The most mature and understanding woman on earth can become a candidate for a mental ward during a break-up.

ful, romantic woman if there was any chance of resolving things. Six months later, I was thankful she had broken up with me—the vile, fickle, crazy creature.

The most mature and understanding woman on earth can become a candidate for a mental ward during a break up. Conversely, the most childish woman on earth can suddenly turn understanding on you, just when you had planned a dramatic scenario to get rid of her. I've seen it all: blackmail, suicide threats, midnight phone calls, public screaming, theft, denial of reality, and more.

When I am the person who breaks off the relationship, I become very busy. I have been known to come down with a real migraine five minutes before a date. The "We have to talk" stage is about as comfortable as having splinters driven under my fingernails. Part of me always delays the break up to the very last moment, thinking, "What if no one ever loves me again?" It's also embarrassing to have become known among my friends for relationships that average two months in length.

But, in spite of what people go through during a break up, they often reach the stage of "polite conversation." Perhaps a date is arranged a month later to offer reassurance . . . but also to give sweet stings. Frankly, I harbor resentments for the hideous methods that have been used to dump me and these polite interactions have led me to believe that outright warfare would be kinder and more honest.

There is much controversy over which is worse: to dump or to be dumped. I heal more quickly and retain much more dignity as the dumper. I swore I would never do it, but as the dumpee, I have begged; I have spent hours in a near catatonic state, alternately placing my hand on the phone and pulling it back. I have wept

19

for days; my bedroom has become a shrine for her pictures; I have "accidentally" driven by her house regularly; and I have slept with her old T-shirt because it was all I had left.

As the dumper, once the dump is over I feel a little guilty, but primarily I feel relieved.

Have you ever noticed that there has to be a reason for a break up? "Things just didn't work out," doesn't resolve things when she's standing there asking, "Why?" Your friends want to know what happened too. So you make something up.

In the beginning, even if you farted, it was cute. This turns into, "Your presence in a room wilts flowers." Neither view holds up under close scrutiny. The reasons women have given for leaving me, although obviously absurd, have been defended beyond rationality. Remember, it doesn't matter if it's true or not, there just has to be a reason.

Personality by Pet

IT'S EASY TO tell what a lesbian is like by the kind of pet she owns. In fact, personality by pet is a science as accurate as astrology, as Tarot cards or numerology. To begin with the broadest categories, there are dog lesbians and cat lesbians. Let's take dog lesbians first. Owners of large vicious dogs are clearly the paranoid type. Generally these women are rough, macho—the female version of G. Gordon Liddy. But you can't always be sure. Don't think you've spotted a killer doberman's owner until you have met the woman's dog face to face. I personally have dated more than one tough leatherette only to find that her dog's name was Cuddles and she spoke baby talk to it.

Then there is the lesbian who owns a sloppy, messy or offensive dog. These women should be approached with caution for they may have a lot of secret hostility which their pet is expressing for them. Are they laughing inside when their dog farts in your face, drools on your suit or mates with your leg? I think so.

Puppy people, on the other hand, are fun, spontaneous types. Unfortunately, they also often lack follow through and responsibility. These are the women who are charmed by a puppy, buy him impulsively and then are never around to train or take care of him. The animal's clean-up, happiness and very survival are left to

Never eat an unexamined hors d'oeuvre at a bird owner's house.

friends, parents and roommates . . . until the next puppy appears.

Athletic dog owners are a hearty breed. I can understand jogging with your dog, but I draw the line at teaching it sit-ups. On the whole this group is tanned, muscular and outdoorsy. They probably even like camping.

Easiest to spot is the dog trainer. These are people whose entire lives revolve around their dogs, not you. Their dogs did not learn that model behavior by themselves. To have a well-trained animal you must spend lots of time with it and these people do, eventually developing Barbara Woodhouse's beaming smile and high-pitched voice. They may ask for dates by asking you if you want to go for "walkies." And it is not just dog owners—I can tell when my lover has been around the cats too much when she begins scratching me behind the ears.

Which brings me to the short but pleasant subject of cat owners. Cat owners are wonderful people. They are mature enough not to need an animal that grovels at their feet. Cats have their own mind and say "No more of that," to you and mean it. A cat takes a command in a tongue-in-cheek sort of way, as if to say, "All right, I won't shred the draperies . . . now."

I have always found it sad that some people cage small furry creatures, or encase gerbils in small plastic balls. I refuse to speculate on tarantula owners and lizard owners. And if someone owns a snake I prefer to believe that they need it for their exotic dancing and don't just like to see rodents swallowed whole.

It seems like every bird owner I've ever known has left the cage door open allowing the creature to fly where it will and poop indiscriminately. Bird poop may be smaller and less smelly, but it's still poop. Such people seem to become impervious to standard social customs and used to poop, which is why I, for one, never eat an unexamined hors d'oeuvre at a bird owner's house.

The independent no-pet type can still be read. There are three reasons to be petless, and a few questions will clear up which category a woman is in. First is the practical reason: moving too much, against apartment rules, severe allergy. This type tends to be pragmatic and reasonable. Secondly, there is the type that is too busy and can't be bothered. Beware of this as a symptom of type A behavior and a high stress level. Lastly is the tragic loss type. This woman can't get over having lost Buttercup, so she'll never have another pet again. This type tends toward melodrama and lives in the past.

And, speaking of melodrama, how sad that we should take on some of the less appealing characteristics of heteros. I am speaking of the "dog as baby substitute" lesbians. My Aunt May has a cocker spaniel named Cookie who sleeps on satin pillows on "his" couch and eats bon bons, after which Auntie brushes his teeth so he won't get cavities. (Truth is stranger than fiction.) Suspect any lesbian of this behavior who buys doggy sweaters or booties. I sometimes suspect my lover of these traits. She has begun to slip the cats salmon leftovers and buys them expensive kitty treats. She regards my demand that the cats eat just cat food with horror, as if I were suggesting kitty torture.

Note: For your own personality by pet analysis, just send money and a description of your pet (or why you don't have one) and you will receive an in depth analysis by return mail.

Who Knows?

I THINK THE words that fill me with the greatest paranoia are—"I could tell you were a lesbian." I immediately run to the nearest mirror to see if there is a lavender "L" on my forehead. I examine my haircut, my dress and posture. Although frequently public about being a lesbian, I never intend to look like what a straight person considers a lesbian to be. There are still situations in which I feel much safer being the one to choose when and who I tell, rather than having them just know. My image of a highly identifiable lesbian to a straight person is a butch in flannels and a crew cut. There are many other kinds of lesbians, but their attire is more subtle, and I have often found that straights who pride themselves on being able to "spot one" miss subtlety. So how do they know?

I finally figured out that people can tell you are a lesbian, not by how you dress and look, but by what is missing. One person I know identified by her resume: "single woman in her thirties, never married." Those of you who work with straight women know what I mean when I say that ninety percent of them are obsessed with the topic of men and relationships. The absence of such talk identifies you as unusual. "I don't know what it is," said a friend's new co-workers, "but there's something different about her."

"Brother, are you barking up the wrong tree!"

In my work with straight women over the years I have found their worst fault to be an obsession with match-making. Lesbians often declare themselves as single even when they are in a relationship with a woman, so they are a major target for these match-makers. There are many defensive tactics I have used over the years to deal with this onslaught. Of course, the most effective way is to tell them; but I am the first to admit that there are situations in which this is not an intelligent choice if you value your career. The easiest dodge I ever had was when I was married. Some women, especially those I've met who are in the military, use marrying a gay man as an effective way of allaying suspicion and obtaining benefits. If you are married, says the military mind, you could not possibly be gay. Lesbians with children, I'm sure, face the same hetero stereotyping.

Sometimes telling women I have herpes is enough to cut off the match-making ritual, but all too often these days they know men who have herpes also.

Far and away the most successful tactic used to maintain my privacy has been the "change the subject tactic." With some straight women, all you have to do to avoid the subject of who you are dating is to ask her about her love life. This is really what she wanted to talk about anyway, so you will be amazed at how many years you can get by with it before she realizes that you have shared only vague and superficial things about your own life.

Other methods of avoiding the topic involve either lying or isolation. I use them only as a last resort because they have sad consequences. I am a terrible liar anyway. As a counselor I have spent too many years indoctrinated with the belief that denial and lying create neurosis to be any good at them.

Another way lesbians stand out is the way they interact with men. Most straight women are prone to let men do the shit work. I was perfectly willing to let my husband do the car mechanics, plumbing and other yucky grunt work. But now that I'm a lesbian I don't like to have to deal with either the protective or the sexual motives of men. So I do it myself.

Lesbians, I believe, do not look for male approval to the extent that straight women do. Whether they are aware of it or not, lesbians tend to cut off the subtle flirtations that men are used to having women respond to. I am not saying lesbians don't get along with men; but when they do it is often more straightforward and sometimes more confrontive. So many times straight men sat across from me in my office trying to manipulate me by flirting with me while I thought to myself, "Brother, are you barking up the wrong tree!"

Add all these differences up and, even if you look like Marilyn Monroe, some enlightened person may put it all together. Due to the confessions of those lesbians who "pass" more and more straights are beginning to realize they are surrounded.

A Lesbian Household

IN PART THIS is a story about Felix the wonder mold, and in part, it is a documentary of living in a lesbian household. Felix hangs, first like a shadow of grey fur, then like a thick black mossy mass on the ceiling of our bathroom. We have beaten him back with everything from Ivory soap to X-14 industrial strength mold killer; the results are temporary. In a house with four women and their assorted lovers, in a bathroom never designed or vented for showers, Felix thrives. Like other group households we wait until one of us reaches the breaking point before attacking him. The last time it was because Tif found a Felix growth on her toothbrush that we heard the warrior cry: "I'm going to kill that mold!"

The bathroom isn't the only disaster area. Our refrigerator has been so well packed with food for the last two years that I have yet to see its inner walls. On occasion, one of us will whiff a strange scent while standing near the fridge and begin the long investigatory process known as the "What on earth is it?" game. Through this game I have come to know how an avocado looks wedged between rack spokes after four months, or how a head of lettuce disintegrates into a black ball of mush two inches in diameter. Many items go beyond the point of recognition.

"Those can't be avocadoes!"

What can I say about the perpetual problem of cleaning? No group house escapes the dishes piled in dangerously tottering masses, while everyone denies having dirtied them. But we have hit on a solution. If the house gets too dirty, we throw a party. Everyone becomes motivated to vacuum, wash dishes and scrub sinks so others don't think we are slobs.

Technically, I have three roommates. In reality, my house is a holiday hotel for lovers and extended friendships. It is also a central location for lesbian potlucks and parties. There is an element of excitement to getting up in the middle of the night and watching unknown naked bodies streak by. I no longer pay attention to strangers unless they have been placed in my bed on a night I was not expected home. Anywhere from one to sixteen may join me at breakfast on the weekend. When I invite someone new over there is a 50-50 chance they have already been there as a party guest or lover of one of my roommates. They know the way.

Shower scheduling is a sharp point of contention. Everyone, ideally, wants a morning shower and there is a limit to the hot water. I have taken to rising at dawn, both for some private time and so that I am assured of a complete hot shower. Standing in line to use the bathroom is a thing of the past. I have grown comfortable with people coming in or out of the bathroom while I'm in the shower—whether I know them or not.

What can be more difficult than lack of physical privacy is the lack of emotional privacy. Some of my women friends have been asked if they were staying the night, long before I was ready to invite them. Other women I have dated (whom I foolishly told my roommates I've had a crush on) have arrived at my door to be greeted with wolf whistles and cheers. There is only a partial solution in going to a lover's house; it doesn't prevent my being greeted the next morning by a line-up of arm-crossed lesbians dying of curiosity and demanding, "Where have you been?" When my house-mates answer the phone and it's my latest crush, there is a certain tone of voice that I know carries to the caller—"Gail . . . it's *her!*"

But for all my despair at living in what sometimes seems like a lesbian sorority, I can't imagine living elsewhere. I love my roommates. We are basically responsible, independent adults who function in a house without rules, with shared food and completely different schedules (not to mention personalities). Contrary to odds, we've been together two years now.

We form the tightest bonds with one another during the winter months when the thermostat is turned to just above freezing and the only sources of additional heat are the fireplace, one lone electric heater and *my* electric blanket. It is during these months that a roommate is not just a roommate. She is a potential source of heat.

Lesbian Potlucks
Through History

I'VE GONE TO so many potlucks since I came out that I once threatened to write a cookbook called "1,001 Things to Make for a Lesbian Potluck." They're such egalitarian events—they enable everyone to prepare according to their abilities and to receive according to their needs. A few years ago there were much stricter rules for the dishes acceptable at potlucks: they had to be vegetarian, made from womyn-grown products, and have redeeming social value. Now we are a much more diverse community. Not only are there vegetarians, there are meat eaters, gourmets and even people who enjoy white sugar (I mention no names).

I'm thankful for the change. I, for one, have eaten enough beans and tofu. But I do feel some nostalgia for those early potlucks which went beyond the above criteria to include intense rituals of chanting, dancing and reciting poetry before food could be consumed. These potlucks were held during the full moons of autumn in the years when I belonged to a small coven and most of my lesbian friends were healers, mystics and hippies. I swallowed gallons of carrot juice, fasted, never touched meat or sugar, and read astrology charts and Tarot cards. (You see, I keep nothing from you about my checkered past.)

Food, I suspect, has played an important role in les-

Tofushu: The Goddess of Lesbian Potlucks

bian history. Many a French lesbian may have been seduced over a seemingly innocent plate of hors d'oeuvres at what was then called a salon but what we now know was a potluck. And perhaps a study should be funded on the role of chocolate in the evolution of lesbianism. Chocolate just happens to contain phenylethylamine, a chemical known to cause a euphoria identical to infatuation. Was it a chocolate croissant that inspired Renee Vivien to write, "I love your carnal lips lingering, still creased by kisses from before . . ."? I think so.

But the history of lesbian potlucks goes much farther back than the French salons. My own favorite part of lesbian history is the age of the great harems of Persia and India. In these harems, a wife rarely saw her husband unless she was a favorite. So what did women do to entertain themselves? Of course, they had lesbian potlucks. They also developed the art of bellydancing, of which I am a devotee. Those present day critics who claim that bellydancing was done only to entice men obviously are unaware that the stages of a woman's life are represented in each part of the dance, and that the cane and sword dances are deliberate parodies of men.

I can see I'm going to have to rewrite history. And why not? The men have.

Going even farther back, I believe there must have been a goddess of lesbian potlucks somewhere amid the Assyrian, Egyptian, or Greco-Roman deities. I mean, they had deities for everything else! The farther back in time you go the stronger the women deities become (see Ishtar, Isis, Kali). Somewhere in there was a lezzie, probably hidden by male misinterpretation or misguided piety on the part of male historians.

It's not easy trying to reclaim the history of lesbian

potlucks. My anthropology teacher never told me about Margaret Mead's lesbianism, much less about cults and ancient societies. What do we even know about Lesbos? Not much. Would Elizabeth Taylor play Sappho in a major motion picture? Never—and that's where most of us learn our history.

Well, some things are changing—maybe Meryl Streep will play Sappho one of these days.

Confessions
Of A Baby Dyke

I WILL ADMIT to you now—I was a baby dyke. My earliest memory of a woman other than my mother is of breasts bursting from a neighbor's dress. Oh, how I loved to stare at women—they seemed softer, more gentle, more erotic than men. By my first few years of grade school I had become adept at sketching women. My brother had given me a learn-to-draw book and to my great pleasure I found that in the back were pictures of women in bathing suits. I traced over them, eliminated the bathing suits and drew in the natural forms. Unfortunately, my mother, ever diligent in her search before laundry time, found those drawings of naked women in my pants pocket. I lied my way out of it saying they must be my older sister's because they were much better than I could ever draw; and my mother believed me. Little did she suspect what talents (in certain areas) I was developing.

It was not long before I graduated from art to real live, full fledged, teacher lust. I clearly recall the light blue sweaters my second grade teacher wore. In those days women's bras drew attention to the conical shapes they held women's breasts in. I was fascinated. At home I stuffed handkerchiefs into my little bikini top and marched around thrusting out my chest, hoping to make my own conical breasts grow. My first true erotic

The day I told my mother I was gay she simply said, "I know."

experience was when my teacher hugged me goodbye at the end of the year and I sank into the soft, warm, perfumed down of her sweater, in between her breasts.

I was a tomboy. I refused to play with the dolls my mother bought me year after year. I proclaimed loudly at an early age that I would never marry a man or have babies, and was furious that no one believed me. I followed my brother everywhere, wanting to be like him: tall and strong, able to do interesting things, not "girl things."

By the time I reached puberty, school sorely tested my capacity to cope. We *had* to wear nylons and girdles (or so we thought). I wasn't very interested in boys. I wasn't in love with one of the Beatles or the Monkees. I developed a crowd of girlfriends who weren't terribly interested in boys either, and we all hung around horses and each other instead.

When one of the girls in my class told me that Richard (a popular boy) liked me, I thought: So what? I could not have cared less about Richard, I had fallen once again into teacher lust. My drama teacher was the most beautiful woman I had ever seen. Despite the fact that I had never been on a stage before, I was determined to devote my entire future to acting. I was shy and introverted and only thirteen, but I tried out for and got the lead in the school play. And I savored my reward—a full semester working closely with Miss Laurenson.

The next year my best friend was a year and a half older than me. And she loved me. We rode on midnight rides in the same saddle, we slept in the same bed at each other's houses and took every opportunity to snuggle against each other's shoulders. We were inseparable; except that she was also heavily into boy lust.

Although I didn't entirely repress the true scope of my feelings, I knew better than to tell her my fantasies. Perhaps because I didn't associate myself with being a lesbian, I didn't think it was unusual that I dreamed of kissing her, or that I identified with the male lead in the movies I saw. I never cared about boys and dating, but I simply thought this was because I was more mature than the other girls, and I did my best to hang out with adults to prove it.

I began acting in an adult theatre company, and fell in love with nearly every beautiful leading lady who would befriend me. They helped me live in an adult world, far from the petty issues of boys and dating. I did some awkward things. I brought flowers to the star of our local production of *Camelot* and I bought her gifts. I lavished far too much attention on my Aunt Pansy, a lovely Southern belle. (I still have an extremely soft spot for southern women.) And I often made the mistake of telling my high school girl friends I loved them.

All this and it never occurred to me that anyone noticed anything. The day I decided to tell my mother I was gay, I was trembling with anxiety. But she simply said: "I know."

"How could you know?" I demanded.

"I watched you grow up," she replied.

Summer Fever

I KNEW IT was going to be one of those days when I began getting an erotic thrill from eating my yogurt: pink, succulent and creamy. I looked out the window of my office and it was sunny. Mount Rainier looked like a blue breast in a white lacy bra. I was lightly sweating. Beads of perspiration clung between my breasts. I called my lover and told her I was thinking about making love to her. It didn't help. We wouldn't have any real time together for another week.

During the business meeting I began to draw curves on a blank sheet of paper. My mind wandered and I could feel silly, inappropriate looks appearing on my face. I had a bad case of hot day dreaminess.

I really believe people should be excused from work during the summer. There are too many months here in Seattle when the clouds hang over us like grey anesthetic cotton and it's my opinion that, like children, we should reserve the cool, rainy, winter months for serious business and save summers for play. Just think of the cruelty of it all—during our childhood years we experience summer freedom, then, suddenly, we're older and two weeks is all we get and that barely gives us time to get the laundry done.

I have to squeeze my hiking, swimming, running and socializing into nights and weekends. After one mara-

I knew it was going to be one of those days when I began getting an erotic thrill from eating my yogurt—pink, succulent and creamy.

thon I nearly had to be carried up the stairs to my office Monday morning. (You see it isn't fair for employers either.) There are even weekends I miss altogether. Between cleaning, ironing, sweeping, tackling the week's dishes and cleaning the bathtub, the hours disappear. I spend some Saturday mornings, eyes glazed over, unable to decide what to start on because it all needs doing.

How romantic can I be when I work all summer? Not very. "Let's see, two weeks from now I have a Saturday, but lets get in early, I have a meeting Sunday morning with the society of left-handed lesbians with anti-political feelings anonymous. Keep in touch in case anything comes along sooner." Or, "I'll be in bed soon, I just have to get this report done, my dress ironed, the cats fed, my overdue bills paid . . . I'd love to make love— zzzzz."

Just try, on a tight schedule, to pick up flowers for a date. There's a line at the only florist who's open, the grocery store bouquets look dead, so you give up, strip your neighbor's rose bush, and try not to notice aphids crawling up her arm as she admires them.

I long for lazy days, long slept into, my lover next to me. I want time to explore ocean beaches. Time to watch the slugs perched in my Brussels sprouts (which I will never eat now). Time to wipe the mold off the bathroom ceiling. Time to write! I could finish my set of erotic humorous lesbian science fiction tales that no one will publish. In short, time to get down to the really important things in life.

Children have 6 to 7 more hours of dream sleep than adults. Scientists think they need these extra hours to make sense of all the data and emotions they absorb during the day. Perhaps all we really need to create a more peaceful and integrated world are summers off to catch up on our dreaming.

The Yearly Exam

IT'S THAT SEASON again. No, I don't mean summer; it is time, once again, for a visit to the gynecologist. Perhaps some of you understand why getting my annual pap smear is not the most joyful of occasions for me. Just as I sincerely feel that men ought to be the ones who get pregnant and go through labor, I also feel they should be the ones who lie on the table on their backs each year, heels high in cold metal stirrups, a sheet covering the top of them and breezes blowing over the exposed lower portions. (For men who do not know: the sheet also acts as a screen so that you cannot see what the doctor is doing down there.) It is an unusual feeling in the best of circumstances. Lights shine so brightly you feel the heat; the doctor mumbles. He or she takes out a speculum which is either cold (wow!) or warmed, either dry (ouch!) or lubricated. Hopefully, since you cannot see, the doctor will describe what he or she is doing. Hopefully, a male intern will not say (as one did) when he is about to insert the speculum: "Here I come."

The speculum has a nasty metallic sound when it opens, but that is nothing to the sound it makes closing, like thin metal scissors coming together, "Oh please," I pray, "do not take skin." Once the inner skin has been scraped and I *do feel* it (contrary to the opinion of one

45

Women who truly seem to love their work.

doctor who assured me that women had no sensory nerves there), the speculum is removed, and the doctor puts on the rubber glove. It is an awkward feeling to have some straight woman or man poking their fingers deep inside you, asking if anything hurts. By then you have been so violated the breast exam is nothing. I do notice they never look you in the eye while doing it. (I do wish my nipples wouldn't go hard no matter who is touching them.)

I usually tell doctors that I am a lesbian. It is not a form of masochism on my part to come out to a possibly prejudiced and almost-never-comfortable-about-the-issue-of-lesbians *person*. It is to avoid being told I have miscarried when I have bled too hard or avoid being told that I must have tried to abort myself if I am hemorrhaging, and it is to avoid being force-fed birth control. I watch their reaction carefully. Usually I get a blank look and a clinical statement that they are not prejudiced. I get the distinct feeling they wish I were not one of their patients.

I do not encounter these reactions in neighborhood women's clinics. In these clinics one encounters women, both straight and gay, who truly seem to love their work. They talk to you, warm and lubricate the speculum, do their best to educate you further on sexuality and the ways your body operates. I do think they get a little carried away when they bring in the mirror so I can look at my cervix or call in others to look at my cervix. Rather than celebrate my womanhood, at that point I would simply prefer they removed the speculum as soon as possible. They do look at me while giving a breast exam, say, 'Gee, I don't know what this is," and soon everyone is feeling my breasts—but I'm open to it. A second opinion is much preferable to a mammogram, which is rather akin to having your boobs squashed in a waffle iron.

This year I'm more at ease. There are gay and lesbian doctors out there and I have one. My yearly pap and exam are still nothing to celebrate, but at least they are nothing to dread. In a caring setting I can ask the embarrassing and hopelessly naive questions I need to ask. I prefer private physicians because of the dignity and privacy of the setting; a woman's clinic is my second choice. I do remember one hospital clinic where I was given a prescription to fill. I went downstairs to the crowded hospital pharmacy, handed in my prescription and sat down with the other patients. A woman from behind the counter shouted, "Sausser, what clinic did you get this from?" I tried to say quietly, "The fourth floor clinic." Then she said, "What?" and everyone was staring at me. After attempting to say it quietly once more I gave up and shouted, "The V.D. Clinic!" So much for privacy.

Gays Need Better P.R.

IN THIS AGE when everything is promoted and commercialized (certainly heterosexuality has been), what gays have lacked is a good public relations agency. We need a new commercial image. The time is right: fashion for women is very butch with suits, ties and fedoras, the straights are copying our lip syncs, and the new men's fashion is skirts—all evidence that we are becoming the dominant culture.

The P.R. agency can start with the press—imagine what a story like "Lesbian and Lover Have Ten Orgasms a Night," would do in the gossip rags, or "Woman Becomes Lesbian after Encounter with Aliens." The women's magazines could run features like "What Lesbians Can Teach Straights about Sensuous Love." The medical journals could be encouraged to publish research findings like "Gays Who Come Out Show Fewer Emotional Problems than the General Population." A family magazine could print "How I Worried about Teenage Pregnancy till My Daughter Told Me She Was Gay." I mean, we are the answer to overpopulation, unwanted pregnancy and sexual repression—let's get some credit for it.

We are naturals for the promotion of certain products. Mary Kay could come out with a whole new line of cross dressing cosmetics that are so effective they can

make butch men pass. Underwear manufacturers can claim their foundation garments can make *anyone* look voluptuous: ("I danced all night at a straight disco and no one could tell in my voluptu-form padding.") There are thousands of new product lines possible. Femme, the perfume for women who like women, and Lesbos Lotion ("After a hard day's work you want your hands to be soft for her.") They can make high heels in men's sizes—"queen size" could take on a whole new meaning. Marketers should realize that many gays have more disposable income than straights who have children or single income households. We are at least ten percent of the population and no one has yet exploited us commercially. In fact, we have the makings of a Megatrend—how did John Naisbitt miss us?

He, and they, missed us for a very good reason—they can't seem to utter the word homosexual. The gays one sees on television are really bi-sexual or reform and become heterosexual in the end. The obviously gay characters are denied. In my opinion, Mr. Whipple has got to be a queen, and LaVerne and Shirley are the biggest closet cases I've ever seen. In the comics I've always wondered why Marcie keeps calling Peppermint Patty "sir." And there is no doubt in my mind that Patty is a very butch little girl. Even on the P.B.S. series "Brideshead Revisited," they refused to acknowledge the gay relationship between those two men. I watched William F. Buckley interview the actors from that series. I was sitting on the edge of my chair screaming: "Say it! Will you just say it!"

They didn't.

In spite of the fact that there's no public acknowledgment, all kinds of rumors get around. Would someone find out who is responsible for all the bad P.R. and fire them! We have been blamed for it *all,* from child abuse to the moral deterioration of the country—of several countries—during several centuries. Gayness has been the grandest moral decadence, the farthest extent of evil. I look in the mirror some mornings and say, "Can this person really be the corrupter of mankind? Womankind?" I wish—I mean, of course not!

I'd like the credit for having that much power, but if you really want to find the source of moral corruption, sexual problems, rape and child abuse, you'll simply have to look at straight men. They have all these vices in above the ninetieth percentile. There's just no basis in fact to blame it on us. But *we're* the ones they want to keep from teaching children!

We have always been accused of promoting homosexuality. I think it's time we *did* actually promote it— don't you think it's time for a national taste test?

Hello, I Am A Lesbian

"HELLO, I AM a lesbian," is one of the public speeches I am most frequently asked to make. I have been out for several years and have sometimes worked doing public education for a gay agency. Part of my job is to be invited to attend a group or class (usually with a gay man and a transsexual), and tell people what it is like to be a "typical lesbian." It can be intimidating. I'm usually asked to stand behind a podium or desk in front of the room. So far, I haven't been asked to stand in a display case, although I sometimes expect it. I try to remember to be grateful they are asking *me* the questions and not a straight psychiatrist. And I can understand their curiosity; I believe it's another sign that we have become a dominant influence.

Even when not lecturing, I am known by many in our local social service community to be a lesbian—a fact which is upsetting to some of the other therapists, but I use the same tactic with them that I do with a class. I remain calm and try to educate. I also make it a point to sit next to the homophobes in meetings, say hello, talk to them and in general give them a rotten day. It is cruel I know, but as Aunt Pansy says, "You can kill them with kindness."

Once, before a lecture, I was asked to wait for the "gay male" who would come and escort me to the class-

Will the typical lesbian please step forward?

room. This proved awkward because he and I had not previously met. I didn't look like a lesbian to him and he didn't look like a gay man, so we missed each other and I had to find the classroom alone. The students seemed amazed that we were unable to identify each other: another myth smashed.

Why people choose to be gay seems to be a major question. As if one morning each of us stood in front of the mirror and said, "I think I'll become a persecuted minority today." They don't realize how much energy most of us expended trying not to be gay until we had to accept it. The next most frequently asked question has to do with why gays flaunt themselves. To these questioners, it makes sense for gays to stay in the closet so straights never need to feel uncomfortable. They forget that it is normal for human beings to talk about their relationships and they fail to see the surfeit of heterosexual ads and public affection as heterosexual flaunting. Another question is why the women all want to look like men and the men want to look like women. Again, this stems from the incredible heterosexual delusion that they can tell by appearance who is gay and who is not.

I have most often found that when I am personable and comfortable, and present a non-judgmental attitude towards their questions, a lot of fearful people loosen up. Men have talked about their fears and their awkwardness in being friendly to gay men, students have come out to their classmates in the middle of our discussion, quiet voices have confessed afterwards that they, "used to hate lesbians." Mostly what I end up talking about is myself, as I have no idea what the "typical lesbian" is like.

Over time I have become increasingly comfortable

with these sessions. No audience or group is all hostile, all straight, or all anything. Even in the presence of professors who look like they are afraid to touch me, or students or colleagues who think they are in the presence of Satan, I obey Aunt Pansy's rule of social grace: "If you remain charming, you make your opponent look like an asshole."

A true southern lady, Aunt Pansy has always been a master of the personal touch. She always stood her ground, but gracefully and kindly. The older I get, the more I wish I were like her.

Movie and T.V.
Heart-Throbs

I LOVED ROMANTIC movies when I was a teenager. I unconsciously identified with all the heroes who got the girl. Since I came out, however, my identifications have changed. Now I yell, "No, no, not him!" at the heroine and root for her female roommate. What a difference a decade (or two) makes. Realizing I am not hetero has really taken the interest out of boy meets girl movies. Or perhaps it is modern movies themselves that have taken the joy out of heterosexuality. If that's romantic love, give me celibacy anytime.

Movies tended to be funny and romantic in my formative years. My dreams and visions of the perfect woman were summed up by Catherine Deneuve's sweet smile and gentleness in *The April Fools.* I saw that movie six times. Catherine replaced an earlier heart-throb of mine. Be honest now, if you are over thirty and a lesbian, didn't you go to see *The Sound of Music* at least twelve times to drool over Mary Poppins—I mean, Julie Andrews?

If I mention long hair, leather jump suit and a Lotus Elan, can you guess my other teen obsession? Emma Peel! The last episode of *The Avengers* tore my heart out. I ran crying from the room when it was over and my parents couldn't figure out what was wrong with me. How could I tell them I'd lost Emma! To this day I will

I also had a crush on Morticia Addams.

watch anything that Diana Rigg is in. I even paid $25 a seat to see her in that made-for-disaster musical *Colette.*

I also had a crush on Morticia Addams (Carolyn Jones) of *The Addams Family.* You've got to love a woman who has pet man-eating plants and only lets her husband kiss her hand. All right, I confess I also liked Doris Day, but only when she played Calamity Jane and wore a tight leather outfit and rescued women.

Do you remember *The Patty Duke Show?* Patty's charms never overwhelmed me, but I do know certain lesbians who were in love with her. I loved Elizabeth Montgomery on *Bewitched,* but like her mother, Endora, I never could understand what she saw in "Derwood." Barbara Eden on *I Dream of Jeannie* was another crush of mine, no matter how politically incorrect her role was. It is amazing to think of the latter two women's roles: both had incredible magical powers, but chose to be subservient to bumbling men who ordered them around. And speaking of politically incorrect, I won't mention the name of the person who had a crush on Tina Louise a.k.a. "Ginger" on *Gilligan's Island,* but I do see it as a forerunner to her current crush on Joan Collins.

One of the most enjoyable rap sessions I ever attended focused on whom everyone had a crush on. A lot of names were mentioned that you would expect: Jane Fonda, Lily Tomlin, Suzanne Pleshette, etc. But the interesting thing was that women confessed to crushes on people like Carol Burnett, Katherine Hepburn at any age, Ellen Goodman the columnist; in general a lot of people were admired and loved for reasons other than physical beauty. Someone even had a crush on Elizabeth Kubler Ross, the death and dying therapist. But women and their crushes on their therapists is an entire essay in itself and I need not go into it here.

I'd like to encourage women to make more movies and put romance back into them again. If anyone has a script, I'd be glad to co-star with Catherine Deneuve in a funny, gentle, sentimental love story about two women who meet, fall in love and live happily ever after.

Personal Habits

WHEN I MOVED in with her bringing only a guitar, chest and clothes she looked at me in horror and said, "That's it?! No dishes? No furniture? No stuff? . . ." To a devout packrat my lack of possessions was unbelievable. I, on the other hand, sell or give away anything I am not currently using. She looked at me with tears in her eyes and asked if I would get rid of her the way I rid myself of possessions. Packrats take my way of living personally.

That was only the beginning of many things we were to discover about one another while living together. Regardless of what you would like her to believe about you while you are dating, living together eventually brings out your less attractive side.

She and I grew up in different generations. I grew up in an age of cheap energy, in the shadow of Hanford's reactor. She grew up in an age of conservation and concern over shortages. I turn on all the lights in the house and leave them on until I go to bed. In one household I was followed by conservers from room to room. If I went upstairs to the bathroom I would find the entire house blackened upon my descent. "I wasn't done down here," I would scream, clawing at the wall for a light switch. I also despise being cold and have had the misfortune of living with people who camp in igloos for

Oh yeah sure . . . a real morning person!

fun and fresh air. I have had to beg (or sneak) the thermostat above 55 degrees. I cannot relax in a living room in which I must wear mittens and ear muffs.

People of my generation, I am told, also waste water. It is not unusual for me to begin brushing my teeth, turn the water on and roam around combing my hair, starting the coffee and putting on a sock before I finally take the toothbrush out of my mouth and shut off the water. If anyone else turns off the water during my meanderings I yell, "I wasn't done yet!" My lover, however, runs only enough water to dampen the toothbrush, shuts off the faucet, brushes, stays over the sink, briefly rinses her mouth and is done. She takes five minute showers. I don't believe I'm clean until my skin puckers.

Our differences in personal habits don't end with our attitudes on conservation. She doesn't watch T.V. I turn it on for company and background noise. I also watch it while bathing. I eat with the refrigerator door open, munching from a half dozen ready to eat foods. She actually cooks. I dislike doing dishes so I drink from cartons, prefer finger food, and if I must, use a single fork or spoon. I have learned to eat leftovers cold and like them. What she eats, she prepares. A full complement of dishes and utensils are used. Even if she only eats a cookie it goes on a plate to catch crumbs—I figure crumb removal is what the cats are for.

It's amazing how many illusions you try to sustain while dating. When you first get together she may pretend to be a morning person too, till one morning you find her slumped in her cornflakes. She may pretend not to watch T.V. (which is how I ended up installing a T.V. in the bathroom and taking two hour baths during prime time). She pretended not to be a sugar junkie till I found two pounds of frosted animal crackers hidden in the cereal cupboard.

My first impression of her was that she dressed very tastefully. I have since found out that she wears a twenty year old bathrobe of faded blue with a large hole in the rear end.

When you first fall in love nature has a way of insulating you from reacting to these discoveries. This is known as "phase one" of a relationship, wherein everything she does is cute and wonderful. Phase two is when you finally realize that some things have been driving you crazy for the last three months.

I am still, blissfully, in phase one. All of my lover's habits strike me as endearingly human. She, however, must contend with an unusual habit of mine: a tendency to write about myself and those around me. I've given her total editing rights but she's beginning to feel like she needs equal time.

My Bunny Mug

WE ALL HAVE a sense of inviolate space in some aspect of our lives. Some object, some place, some deserved relaxation is ours! In my case I have a bunny mug to drink from. I also insist on reading the comics from the newspaper before anyone else. These idiosyncracies define my territory and give me a sense that all is right in an otherwise disturbed world.

Old Tuna Breath (my dear cat) insists on sleeping between us in bed at about head level. If he is in an affectionate mood he touches my cheek lightly with his paw and breathes heavily into my face (which is how he got his nickname). No amount of effort on our part has trained him out of this habit. He has defined his territory; we can only hope to control his diet more carefully. Cat breath reeking of garlic leftovers is a heck of a way to wake up in the middle of the night.

Sometimes human territoriality is in response to a need. When I come home from a hard day of construction work (yes, sometimes counselors have other jobs, too), there's a good chance I'll consume everything in sight. My lover has learned to insist that certain food items are hers, or to remind me that I am entitled to only half of the casserole.

No one can convince me that people ever grow too mature to fight over the last brownie. From our child-

My Bunny Mug

hood, when we couldn't sleep without our Teddie bear, to adulthood, when we can't sleep without our feather pillow, the territorial instinct continues to motivate us. Having once been a bartender, I know people not only get territorial about their bar and the way they want their drink served, they have a ruined evening if someone else is on *their* barstool.

Certain times of the day cause us to regress to greater territoriality than others. Morning is my lover's "grumpy time." Heaven help me if we're out of orange juice or if I try to read *Forbes* before she's done with it. These days I only know what happened in investments a month ago.

Another aspect of defining one's space is what you will not permit near you. My lover goes into hysterics if tofu comes near her. She so hates the texture, which she describes as akin to cold white liver, that she cannot bear even thinking about it. Neither does she like carob, which she says tastes like brown crayon.

I take classes at a community college and I have noticed that in the first night's rush to find a seat, we have defined where we will sit for the rest of the quarter.

Something no good feminist feels any more is territoriality in relationships. But no matter how much we mature, there are still inklings of jealousy and possessiveness. When they arise, I think of them as being on the same level as my need to drink from a bunny mug—just a sign of some basic insecurities coming to the surface. It is odd that most people assume that we are more jealous and possessive than we are. Singles express fear of interrupting us; at dinner parties we are seated together; and we are almost never asked to do anything separately. Now our invitations are addressed to GailandFriend, not to two separate people. Most of that is understandable. Too much of it is irritating. Listen, I can still be asked to dance, go to events alone and bear the company of a third woman without thinking my relationship is threatened. Give me some credit. Now, as for drinking from my Bunny Mug—that's entirely a different matter.

"Do You Prefer Cuddling To The Act?"

ACCORDING TO THE Stoddard Institute, a highly reputable sexual study foundation, the average heterosexual sex act lasts two minutes in length and has very little to do with cuddling. (During the "sexual revolution" it was even shorter: one minute, twelve seconds.) As Ann Landers found, women overwhelmingly prefer cuddling to the "act." And a male columnist suggested men may prefer Monday night football to all of the above. (Although commercials during the game are about two minutes.) Poor hetero women!

Can't you just picture thousands of reluctant women saying, "No," then, "Oh well, get it over with." Have males learned nothing about pleasing? True, when I was involved with men I suspected that they were just using my body to masturbate with, but I also thought that part of it was that I was really a lesbian and shouldn't have been there in the first place. Now that science has proved my experiences are the mode, why do hetero women put up with it? To be perfectly frank, I can't get off in two minutes, and I don't know any women who can. No wonder straight women have so many pre-orgasmic groups. It sometimes takes me ten to twenty minutes . . . a very wonderful twenty minutes too, I might add. If I am out of bed in under an hour I consider it a quickie.

If I'm out of bed in under an hour I consider it a quickie.

When Pepper Schwartz, co-author of the bestselling book "American Couples," first said that lesbians have less sex than straights or gay men, I was a bit miffed. I even claimed that I knew one woman who, if surveyed, would tip the scale back again. But if this is the quality they are getting I'll take less frequency anytime.

Women are socialized to be shy. We are always supposed to be nice and not hurt anyone else's feelings, i.e., women are trained to be victims. It's not easy for most women to say, "Don't do that," (we might hurt their feelings or their masculine pride). It's not easy to say, "Not there, over here, this is how I like it," (we might make them think they don't know what they are doing). And we really get in trouble for, "Harder!" because that implies a little bit of sexual aggressiveness or perhaps even S&M. But things have gotten outrageous! I want the hetero women to say, "Not on your life buddy, till you listen to me and learn to do it right!"

I surveyed some lezzie friends with Ann Landers' question: "Do you prefer cuddling to the 'act'?" They replied "What do you mean? Cuddling *is* part of the act—sex *is* affectionate!" I surveyed some gay male friends and they said that two minutes had its uses, but they too preferred cuddling *and* sex. I'm not saying gays are better sexually adjusted than straights, but we certainly seem to enjoy it more.

Unfortunately, in the division of roles, straights have made women the cuddlers and men the sex actors, and rarely, evidently, the twain meet. Sorry heteros.

The Love Menagerie

WHILE SOME MAY say that lesbian relationships don't have staying power, I totally disagree. I have seen what women have endured from their lovers' pets and it's a tribute to enduring affection.

It is not tactful to be truthful about people's pets, so let me just say, I know of some dogs (certainly not those of my friends) who reek doggie smell, who claw clothes, hump legs, howl, and either crash into every possession or claw and chew it apart. I have even inherited un-potty trained animals from a lover.

I've known women who have had to put up with apartments that smelled like kennels or kitty litter, cats that slept on their face, kittens that sucked on their necks, tomcats that sprayed their clothes, cat hair in their food, large Labrador bedmates, and more. The owner is oblivious. When a 200 pound Newfoundland dog crawled onto my lap, began dripping hot drool and getting excited, I fought valiantly for space, pounded its head and screamed, "Go away!" The owner said only, "I think he likes you."

My lover cannot live happily without cats. So, naturally, I agreed to acquiring one. I had visions of a warm and cuddly little friend when she suggested that we go to the pound to claim the animal I now have a love/hate relationship with. Quiet and emaciated when we first

Who ever said cats are easy to take care of?

brought him home, he hid in the closet, afraid to come out. We were overjoyed when he uttered his first meow; now we can't shut him up. And his slender figure is a thing of the past. (Lately we call him Meatloaf instead of Old Tuna Breath.) Meatloaf guards the food dish from Oliver, my lover's other cat, and gorges himself. He also gets extremely bitchy when he's hungry and emits a high-pitched yowl that acts as sufficient blackmail to get him all the food he wants.

He has his good points. He is attractive, mellow, unafraid of people and willing to be passed around in a game I call kitty football. He follows me like a large black, purring sausage wherever I go.

Whoever told me cats are quiet pets had never heard the galloping chase that goes on each night as Meatloaf launches himself from our highbacked chair, sending it crashing to the floor. And they most certainly hadn't heard Meatloaf howl!

Whoever said that cats are graceful hadn't felt the quake of our bed under Meatloaf's mighty weight each morning (telling us, of course, that he is hungry); nor had they found themselves rushing Oliver to the pet hospital because he caused a lamp to fall and broke his toe. (Oliver also wallows in such ecstasy on our bed that he forgets there is an edge and rolls off it.)

Whoever said cats are easy to take care of hadn't had to stare at a full kitty litter box each morning or fight its smell.

Whoever said cats are clean had never seen the lumps of kitty chow stuck to Meatloaf's face—lumps he never washes off; nor had they awakened to an apartment of shredded carpets and newspapers and tipped-over plants that had been rolled in.

Upon being introduced to a woman who acquired a

dog, three cats, a parrot and a ferret as her lover's dowry, I could only shake her hand, tears in my eyes, and say, "Such love!"

A Lesbian Housewife

MONEY IS A hard thing to talk about. I stutter and blush when I need to talk to my partner about my financial dependence on her, not when we are trying to clear up some sexual confusion.

When I became a feminist, I accepted a few basic beliefs along the way: 1) I don't want to be dependent on anyone and 2) I have value only as long as I am an independent, working woman. But fate has a way of making us face the actual worth of our convictions. I am now unemployed, in school and living in poverty. The woman I live with, however, can afford to go out to dinner, to the theatre and on occasional vacations. Should I say I can't go, as my previous convictions state, or should I allow my way to be paid? So far I have consistently answered, "I'll go with you," and I have become what a friend refers to as a "K.W." a kept woman—an anathema to feminists and yuppies alike.

In adjusting to my new (and temporary, I hope) unemployed status, I have had to learn a few new concepts. First of all, my lover has let me know that her resources are ours and she prefers not to see me go without anything that I need. Secondly, I have had to look at our relationship as something enduring, ergo, she feels she will benefit from my continuing education. To her, it is an investment in the future. A straight

Every relationship brings up unique issues.

friend in the same position suggested I learn to accept graciously what is given to me in love, allowing the other person the joy of giving support.

In the beginning I promised myself I would pay back every penny. Now my defenses are lower and I realize I like being part of a family style relationship. If roles were reversed, I know I would feel the same way about her—that makes it easier. What makes it harder is that, because of our choice of careers, I will probably never make as much as she does. If, trying to keep up, I do count pennies, I'll have a hard row.

Unemployment gives me more time, so naturally I do most of the shopping, cleaning and cooking. I watch game shows and learn via cable how to use my new Cuisinart and microwave to make tuna fish casserole. Of course, she had to adjust to someone doing all these things for her just as I had to adjust to someone else paying the bills. Frankly, I want to do all the housework so that we can play in the time we do have together. For the time being, I am a lesbian housewife.

Sometimes I am angry that we met at such an unsettled time in my life. But I also know if this hadn't happened we would have kept an economic barrier between us for a long time, and I would never have known how much commitment she feels toward me. But sharing in one another's monetary welfare is a sticky area in which heteros have protection and gays do not. It is for this reason that my lover and I began to discuss wills, beneficiaries and powers of attorney, in addition to a physician's statement that gives the other the power to decide for us in case of accident instead of our relatives. We also discussed an equitable dissolution of our shared possessions if we break up. If it sounds like we are writing a marriage contract and plan for divorce settlement at the same time—we are, with professional legal help.

Many of my friends were happy to see the woman win in the Lindsey vs. Lindsey case. Basically the verdict in Lindsey vs. Lindsey said that the woman owned equally what this heterosexual couple had acquired together before their marriage. This opened up the whole area of benefits for lovers. I am not a lawyer, but it seemed to me that the case held together on two main points. One, they were planning to get married; and two, they were heterosexual—so their marriage would have been legal. I feel strongly that gay and lesbian couples should write contracts stating their plans and intentions for their possessions and not leave it to courts and bereaved relatives. Contracts, unlike gay marriages, are legally recognized.

Every relationship brings up unique issues. Gay relationships are as unique as the people in them. Certainly not all will choose to share economic resources. Many even detest the idea of marriage and see gay marriage as a regression to latent heterosexual role playing. My point is, whatever the relationship, there is a monetary element.

The other day I asked my lover if being a housewife meant I was going to get appliances for presents from now on. She said she was planning on buying me an electric sander. She still knows what I really want! I may be a lesbian housewife, but I'm a butch one.

De-Dyking The Apartment

IT MUST HAVE been the glow of first love that made me forget that if I married someone, even another woman, I would eventually suffer from the primordial plague of in-laws. The day her parents visit is a dreaded day in the life of most lesbian couples. In my case I was told that they would be staying with us for *four* days. (She isn't out to them yet.) After I recovered from the initial shock I began to plan to leave town and visit old friends. When I became somewhat rational again she explained that she wanted me to stay and support her. She wanted her parents to get to know me better and become used to the fact that I was an important part of her life. We began to plan.

One major obstacle is that, while we do have a second room, we have no second bed. And, unfortunately, the second room is the only storage area for skis, boxes, weights, the ironing board, guitars, bicycles and books. How we turned this room into a bedroom is a story in itself. In brief, my advice to others is to compress, borrow a bed, and at least hang pictures on the wall. Then, keep the door closed as often as possible.

I am sometimes curious whether they know or not. There seem to be two viable options. They are either cool and silent about the fact that they know; or they are so dense they will never comprehend anyway. For

The day parents visit is a dreaded day in the lives of most lesbian couples.

instance, if you slip and say, "Here, honey," they will think they heard, "Here's money." Denial is a wonderful mechanism.

De-dyking the apartment is an important preparation. Take the love notes off the refrigerator, remove lesbian books from the bookcase, check to make sure no nude women posters are around and, most vital, check your night stand. They slept in the bed we usually use and there was a moment when I wondered, "Did she remember to remove the flourescent body paints and the love oils?" She had.

I know some may think, "Why play games? Why not tell them?" To begin with, I strongly believe that it is her decision to make, not mine. And there is also the argument that, when you are not close to your parents, they may want to know about your sex life as much as you want to know about theirs. Not much.

The first night I coaxed her off the couch, swearing it is not abnormal for two women to share the same room. I even coaxed her off the carpet where she had obviously placed a sleeping bag, telling her it is not unusual for two women to share the same queen-sized bed. By the third night we even dared practice the strenuous art of soundless lovemaking.

We did make slips. They noticed we referred to the cats as ours. They must have noticed that we kept making excuses to go to the back room (where we were necking). And we referred to trips we had taken together. They also never asked about boyfriends, parenting or marriage. I began to think that the first alternative was true: they knew, but were being silent about it.

After four days of careful behavior on our part, they left. There were no confrontations. Her sisters called afterwards to say their parents had had a wonderful time.

We have seen them since that visit, they have called and kept in touch. The periods when they seem to understand our relationship are very episodic. Some days I could swear they know, but on other days their response is oblivion. On one such day they asked her when she was getting married and told her they wanted grandchildren. She answered very clearly, "I'm never going to marry a man and have children." They said what parents often say to that statement, "You just haven't met the right man yet." It dashed our hopes that they had at least minimal comprehension. Yet, there are other times, like when they sent a Christmas present addressed to both of us, when they seem to be referring to us as a couple.

For those involved in the study of psychology, I believe my in-laws are a fascinating case. The idea of our relationship appears not to stay repressed in denial, but to cascade in and out of their consciousness like a roller coaster. Since their daughter's gayness is unstated, they need only deal with it periodically, like a television channel they can switch in and out of.

They also seem to have a sixth sense that tells them when to back off. After their questions about marriage and children my lover nearly told them, but, apparently psychically sensing they were nearing the truth, they have not brought up marriage since.

Seduction in Perspective

THE WAYS WE signal and attract each other have never ceased to amuse me, especially now that I am married to a woman and can look back on my frantic and awkward dating period with some perspective. Although "catching someone's eye" is a time honored approach, I never found it to do any good. And when I tried to follow this maneuver by starting a conversation I always felt like the female version of Gomer Pyle, "Yup, this sure is a nice evening, yup, yup . . ." After which the woman would walk away and view me suspiciously ever after.

During one era I attempted the "intellectual request" approach to no avail. The "casual touch" approach brought mixed reaction: either it worked or I was viewed with disgust. However, the "casual touch" approach has always been successful with me. A few soft and warm caresses during a slow dance and I would forget she looked like a football tackle for the losing team. Finally, my personal style settled on the "fawning friendship" approach; often ineffective, but nearly always safe.

In fact, if I had one word to describe my style of lesbian seduction it would have to be "denial." From the moment I first began to stare at the moisture on her luscious lips and watch her rear sway as she climbed the

I continued to pretend it was a casual kiss, even though I was having a lip orgasm.

stairs in front of me, I assured her constantly that we were "just friends." I asked her out to all the important events of my life, paid her way, dressed to the teeth, but assured her that we weren't really dating. I spent at least three evenings a week with her and called in between. I finally told her I loved her . . . as a friend. And when she finally kissed me I continued to pretend it was a casual kiss even though I was having a lip orgasm.

Thankfully, the fawning friendship is behind me. Looking back, it's amazing I ever slept with anyone, but I guess in some cases there was so much mutual attraction it battered down my defenses. Not to say that I ever approached the first night without difficulty. Somehow it always seemed more awkward than I had pictured in my romantic visions; as in the night I got up in the midst of making love and locked myself in the bathroom. Or there was the time she wanted to take a shower with me and I made her turn out the lights in modesty. (It was hell when one of us dropped the soap.) But, of course, those incidents happened when I was *much* younger. It takes time to achieve a balance so that you aren't wrestling each other over being the aggressor, or both passively lying there wondering what the other person is going to do. It takes time and teaching.

The next awkward part of the seduction scenario, for me, was that as soon as I slept with someone we became a couple. It usually took only a month before I moved in with them, in spite of the fact that I knew very little about them. The average length of a relationship was very short and I did a great deal of moving.

When I met the woman I married, I once again moved in after a month, but this time we spent an entire evening devoted to "test questions." On the top of her list was, "Did I like cats?" Yes, even before honesty and openness, she placed my reaction to the thought of living with cats, the furry little children of her life. Sometimes these important issues come up casually in a conversation. If you are dating and she suddenly asks if you mind people who eat cold pizza for breakfast, or if it makes you gag—you may wonder, "Is this a test question?" But always be grateful she is asking now and not after you have moved the piano.

The Dreaded Fusion

A BURNING ISSUE these days is fusion in lesbian relationships. (Fusion: the unhealthy melding of two dependent personalities.) It's true that I have a harder time
getting out now that I'm married. I sit at home thinking
that I could go out into the cold rain, drive across town
to a rap group, see several people I know (but mostly
see strangers), or we could have a quiet dinner at home,
cuddle by the fire and make love. Guess which wins?
Even when I do go out, if I know she's at home I begin
edging for the door sooner than I ought to.

I was very social as a single. I went to every party and
event possible. I even lived in a party house. I met some
couples, but basically ignored them. My focus was on
keeping track of who was free and single.

Now I'm the one experiencing rejection when I'm introduced to singles: they like me till I introduce them to
my wife, then they disappear. There are many reasons
people shy away from couples: neither member of the
couple is available so why bother, some think; others
fear one couple member will get jealous, and then
there's always the awkwardness of being a third person.
A couple sitting together appears to be almost a world
in itself. Both my partner and I try to go off singly part
of the time and make a point of talking to others; otherwise no one would talk to us.

The Dreaded Fusion

It's hard keeping track of couple friends. They date each other, go off on weekends. Planned events have to match both of our schedules and both of theirs. If one person from the other couple can't make it, everything is off. Nothing happens spontaneously.

There is another reason we go off singly with friends at times. Couples have heard all their partner's stories a hundred times. They know the events of the day, how their partner feels, what they like. This limits conversation. I can feel great telling a funny story, making people laugh, but I notice my partner falling asleep in the corner, having heard it all before.

Couples also tend to respond emotionally to their partner's comments: "You never told me you felt that way!" "Don't say that in public!" and a favorite from a previous union, "You're embarrassing me!" If you haven't agreed on what information is public and private, mistakes are bound to be made. In my work as a counselor I've gotten used to discussing the most sordid subjects without batting an eye, and I sometimes go too far when I'm out with friends. (If you value your emotional privacy, never marry a counselor . . . or a writer. Luckily, I found someone tolerant of both.)

Often couples define their personalities in contrast to each other: one's a slob, one's neat; one is social, one is shy; one cooks, one fixes things. Sometimes fusion is less becoming alike than it is becoming set in the role you play and whether you compensate for a quality your partner lacks.

On the positive side, fusion can be a phase of a relationship. "Phase One" my friends call it, and are still asking when I'll grow out of it. It's the fascinating and romantic dream you experience when you are in love. I'm not over it so I won't try to guess how long it continues. I do think you can wear it out all at once or keep rekindling it. It is special efforts and kindnesses that keep love going, and smothering that kills it. That's common sense.

It always amazes me that some people enter into relationships with the attitude that now that they are a couple they can dispense with the kindness and personal regard they had for each other previously. They treat their partners rudely, are insensitive to their wants and demanding of their time and effort. Eventually, love dies from neglect and abuse. If that's love, give me the courtesy of total strangers.

I believe a relationship of love can be a healthy fusion. I feel eternally bonded to my partner. On the other hand, though, she's not my entire identity or only friend.

Some call the phase after infatuation the "independence" phase. After you've been obsessed with one another, you reaffirm your personal needs and give each other some space. I find that is happening naturally without any slack in infatuation. Somehow deep bonding and independence are both possible. I've seen enough good marriages to believe it.

I Love Happy Endings

I LOVE HAPPY endings. That's probably why I never used to read much lesbian fiction. Until recently, lesbian fiction has had only two possible endings: loss and eternal depression, and/or suicide. Relationships never worked out and were always the motivating force behind the loss, depression and suicide. I absolutely refused to read *The Well of Loneliness* because of the title.

A good example of what I'm talking about is D.H. Lawrence's novel *The Fox*. It's emotional and genuine, but once you are sucked into caring about these women and their relationship, one of them runs away with a man (the fox), which for some reason connected with fate, causes a tree to fall on the other and kill her (tree being a phallic symbol). It took Rita Mae Brown to get me to read lesbian fiction again.

I have a friend who stands in the bookstore reading the last two paragraphs of every lesbian novel she is considering buying so she can be sure she won't encounter a tragic ending. I've done the same thing. It's not just the desire for the lesbian equivalent of a romance novel. Lesbian relationships and lives *don't* always end in disaster. I'd like to read about those for a change of pace—especially since I, personally, am happily married to my woman soul mate and a tree hasn't fallen on me yet. I want fiction to reflect this other real side of relationships.

And it's certainly not just straights who make up our tragic endings. The gay community at large has a hard time believing in the success of romantic love. (I think we read too much.) In the absence of lesbian models of stability and enduring love, too many have just given up on the idea.

When I first announced my marital intentions I encountered outright hostility in the gay community. Everyone thought I was going to be ripped off and was just creating a hassle for myself because it wouldn't be easy to grab my bags and move on. My response to that is—how can you possibly have a lasting relationship if you never believe it's possible and you keep your bags packed by the door? I married well. I want to be married for keeps and I'm willing to put power of attorney in her hands and all I own. If there are hassles I intend to work them out, not just grab my bags and say, "Next . . ."

I think reading about dismal failure and unhappiness has affected us badly. I think we should examine our underlying assumptions and it might not be a bad idea to read a really romantic lesbian novel now and then— one with a very happy ending.

I love happy endings.